A
MINDFUL
YEAR

HarperCollins*Publishers*
1 London Bridge Street
London SE1 9GF
www.harpercollins.co.uk

First published by HarperCollins*Publishers* in 2019

1 3 5 7 9 10 8 6 4 2

Text by Emma Bastow
Design by e-Digital Design

A catalogue record for this book is available from the British Library

ISBN 978-0-00-837318-4

Printed and bound in China

MIX
Paper from
responsible sources
FSC
www.fsc.org   FSC™ C007454

This book is produced from independently certified FSC™ paper
to ensure responsible forest management.

For more information visit: www.harpercollins.co.uk/green

A MINDFUL YEAR

365 THOUGHTFUL WRITING PROMPTS

About the Author

Emma Bastow lives by the sunny south coast of England, where she is lucky enough to combine her passion for creative writing with a career as a freelance editor. When she's not playing with words or lost in the pages of a book, she can be found skipping stones at the beach with her young son, cooking up a storm in the kitchen, and wandering the lanes of Brighton.

For Marion, with love.

Introduction

Stop. Right now. Stop everything you are doing, put this book down and take a few moments to simply *be*. How was it? Mindfulness is about being completely in the moment. Not fretting about the past or worrying about the future, but simply being in the here and now. And it's not always as easy as it sounds. With heads full of tasks, chores, deadlines, and endless to-do lists, pausing to focus on the present may take a bit of practice. Whether you are new to mindfulness or have already begun your journey, here you will find prompts to inspire you and help to bring your attention to the present moment.

How to use this book

In the following pages you will find 365 prompts for every mood, with space below to note down your thoughts and feelings. You may like to work through the book methodically, allocating a little time each day to developing a mindful practice. Or you might prefer to flick through the book at random, selecting the exercises that take your fancy. However you chose to use this book, be kind to yourself and move on to another prompt if an exercise doesn't feel quite right—with 365 prompts to choose from, there's bound to be an idea a few pages away that will better suit you in this moment.

Getting started

If the idea of training your mind to be more focused on the present seems a little daunting, try this simple meditation to help quiet your thoughts and bring your attention to the now.

- Sit comfortably on the floor or in a chair with your back straight. Let your hands rest in your lap.
- Close your eyes and relax your facial muscles, allowing your jaw to go slack.

- Concentrate on your breathing. Notice how your chest rises and falls with each inhalation and exhalation.
- Allow thoughts to come and go but try not to dwell. Return to focusing on the breath if you feel your mind wandering.
- Stay here for as long as you feel comfortable, enjoying the clarity this simple exercise can bring.

Why be mindful?
Mindfulness can help us to feel calmer and more focused. It can help us to find joy in mundane tasks, teach us to be less judgmental, and allow us to channel negative emotions. And the real beauty is that it can be practiced anywhere with no expense or equipment. Stuck in a traffic jam? Look up and find shapes in the clouds, notice the changing light, and visualize the expanse of space beyond your field of vision. Feeling overwhelmed at work? Step away for a few moments, close your eyes and allow your mind to go quiet before tackling the next e-mail or meeting. Training your mind to be concerned with nothing more than this very second can have the most wonderful effect on your sense of wellbeing—try it and see for yourself!

What would you like to be better at?

What will you let go of today?

Close your eyes and listen to the sounds around you. What can you hear?

What appeals to you more, a spa break on a remote island or a city break with a packed itinerary?

Try changing your daily routine—alter your route to school or work, eat lunch in a different location, try out a new coffee shop. Do you miss the familiarity or has the change opened your eyes?

Take time to exercise today—this could be as simple as walking around the block or taking five minutes to stretch. Note if the period of exercise changes your mood.

Put your cell phone out of sight, allowing yourself to only check it at set intervals throughout the day. Were you able to stick to your own self-imposed limits?

Think about the last time you felt anxious. What would have helped to calm you?

Tell someone you love them. What is their reaction?

Close your eyes and imagine that everything around you is the color yellow. What effect might this have on your mood?

Visualize waves crashing on a beach—hear the roar of the ocean, see the ebb and flow of the water, smell the salty air. Is there a period in your life when you have felt like the waves?

Try out a random act of kindness and note the effects on your state of mind.

Imagine you are an astronaut floating in space looking down at the Earth. How do you feel about the impact humans have had on our planet?

Play a favorite piece of music and dance with abandon. Do you feel self-conscious or liberated? Foolish or happy?

Use the space below to draw a simple picture. Without too much thought, select colors and shapes that appeal to you right now, then consider what the picture says about your mood in this moment.

Write a list of goals for today and tick them off as you complete each task. Is there anything you were unable to complete? Are you at ease with this or frustrated?

Close your eyes and slowly count backwards from ten to zero, focusing on the breath. Open your eyes. Were you able to maintain focus?

What would you like to give up?

How will you focus on slowing down today?

We create our own stress. To what extent is this true?

What would you like to have achieved by this time next year and how will you work towards this?

When was the happiest time of your life? Why was this? Are there any elements from that time you can replicate today?

What is your usual routine on waking—do you jump out of bed immediately or reach for your cell phone? Tomorrow morning do something different.

When was the last time you were really angry? Was this justified?
Re-write the situation to avoid feelings of anger.

Where is your happy place?

What has challenged you today?

When was the last time you said thank you?

Note five things that have brought you joy today.

When did you last spend time alone? If this is a rarity, try to set aside a day to yourself without agenda and see where your mood takes you.

Take time to check-in with yourself at regular intervals. How are you today? What could you change to improve your mood?

Think about the last time you experienced conflict. Were you able to stand your ground or were you overruled? How did this make you feel?

A stranger enters your home and is asked to create a personality profile based on the décor and your possessions. What might they include?

Do you feel comfortable saying no?

Can stress ever be positive?

Try something new today—cook a dish you haven't prepared before, attend a different exercise class, take a walk to an unfamiliar location.

How empathetic are you? Are you aware of the feelings and emotions of those around you?

When were you last outside of your comfort zone? Did you enjoy the challenge?

Think about the passing of time. To what extent do you use time wisely?
Are there any ways you can free up more of your time? And how will
you spend it?

How do you react to change?

Do you like your own company?

Strike up a conversation with a stranger. Does this come naturally to you or does it feel awkward?

To what extent are you an honest person? Is not telling the truth sometimes the best course of action?

The next time you wake in the night with your mind racing, use this space to note down your thoughts. This simple act may be enough to quiet your mind and allow sleep to wash over you.

Think about which colors you are naturally drawn to. Are they soothing, quiet colors or bold and bright? What does this say about you?

Make a list of your achievements, no matter how small. Allow yourself to feel proud and celebrate your successes.

Take time for simple pleasures. This may be a call with a friend, reading a chapter of a favorite book, or soaking in the bathtub. Note if you found this restorative or if you felt rushed due to the busyness of the day.

List five things that have made you smile today.

Who do you most enjoy spending time with?

What are you grateful for?

Do you avoid conflict?

Stand barefoot on a grassed area. How does the grass feel? Is it dry or is there some moisture present? Try scrunching up your toes and standing on tip toes and experience the changing sensations.

Describe someone you dislike using only positive words.

Write a to-do list and include everything you need to get done. This could be for the day, the week, the month, or even the year. How do you feel seeing your tasks on paper? More organized or overwhelmed?

Write a list of things in your life that make you happy. The next time you are in need of a mood booster come back to this list.

Is there a time in your life when you've been able to turn a negative situation into a positive one?

Try eating a meal with your eyes closed. Take time to appreciate the flavors and be aware of the textures. How different was this experience to your regular mealtimes?

Head outside and take a slow walk. Stop after 100 yards or so and return to your starting point. Now follow the same path but this time try running as fast as you can. How did the two journeys compare?

Are you a patient person?

How will you seize the day?

Set aside some time today to be still. Let your body relax and your mind wander. Were you at ease or were you itching to get on with the day?

Do you make snap decisions, or can you be indecisive? The next time you are faced with a big decision, write down all possible outcomes and play the scenarios out in your mind.

Declutter one area of your home or workspace. Retain only the objects that are truly useful or have meaning, and appreciate the order you have created.

Head out to your backyard or local park. Look around at the trees, flowers, and wildlife—all co-existing in this space—and appreciate the wonder of nature.

Draw a picture of the first thing you think of that is associated with the color blue.

How would your friends describe you in five words?

Does luck exist?

Place your hands on your stomach and breathe in. What do you notice as the breath enters your body?

_____

_____

_____

_____

_____

_____

_____

_____

_____

_____

_____

_____

_____

_____

_____

_____

_____

_____

Are you prone to speaking before thinking? Pause and think about how what you are about to say will be received.

Write a list of negative emotions. In the next column, list their positive equivalents. Appreciate that to enjoy the positives, we sometimes have to experience the negatives.

Negative emotions	Positive emotions

Think about the last time you upset someone. Were your actions justified? What did you learn from this experience?

We are said to be creatures of habit. List yours, good and bad.
What does this say about you as a person?

List the first five things that come to mind when you read the following words:

Creation

Symbolism

Migration

Apathy

If you had the power to change one thing about your personality, what would you choose and why?

What was your favorite pastime when you were a child? Can you incorporate some elements of this activity into your life today?

What are you most scared of?

List five things you like about yourself.

How easy do you find it to open up to those around you?

You enter a building and can see two rooms. One is full of people chatting with music playing. The second is empty except for an armchair and a copy of your favorite book. Which room do you enter?

When in your life have you traded short-term gain for a potential longer-term gratification?

In what ways are you investing in your future? This could be from a financial, medical, or educational perspective.

What is the greatest piece of advice you could give a child?

Make a list of compliments you have received from others. What does this say about how you are perceived by those around you?

Think of a time when you have felt criticized. How did it make you feel and how did you react? Would you react in the same way again?

What are your coping mechanisms for when you feel overwhelmed?
Are you able to step back mentally and reassess?

Do you have good intuition?

What time is it? What are you usually doing at this time of day?

What has been your biggest surprise?

What makes you angry?

How good are you at being assertive? Try asking for what you need and note how others react.

What elements need to be present for you to experience true happiness? How many of these can you factor into today?

The next time you feel like things are spiraling out of control, lie down on the ground. Be supported by the ground beneath you and allow your limbs to be heavy. Take a few deep breaths.

Stretch your arms out to the sides. Start to move your arms slowly in small circles, then gradually speed up, making the circles increasingly large. Feel the air rushing through your fingers and notice as your arms tire.

Pick up a vegetable or piece of fruit. Think about how it came into being and its journey from seed or sapling to your hand.

Close your eyes and visualize a box marked "negative thoughts." Imagine writing your negative thoughts on pieces of paper and placing them in the box. Now do the same for "positive thoughts." Which box has the most pieces of paper?

Turn your morning coffee into a mindful ritual. Be aware of the effect of the hot water on the ground coffee, how these two elements unite. Notice the swirls in the liquid as you stir and appreciate how this warming drink makes you feel.

What does the world need more of?

Does anyone know the real you?

What could you not live without? Divide the list into the material and emotional. Which category has the most entries?

Material | Emotional

Set aside a day to be completely in the moment, without distractions from work, e-mails, or television. Let your thoughts come and go but try not to dwell—your focus should be on the here and now.

How are you? All too often we answer this question with "I'm fine,"
even if we aren't. Think about how you really are today.

What does wellness mean to you, and what steps do you take to maintain your own wellness?

Who do you turn to for support? Having a network of trusted supporters around us can be reassuring in times of need.

Think of a necessary chore or activity you really dislike. What is it that you dislike? Are there any steps you could take to make the activity more enjoyable?

Thoughts are not facts. To what extent is this true?

How are you kind to yourself?

If your body could talk, what would it say?

Is there someone in your life you can't forgive? Imagine saying the words "I forgive you" to them. Do you feel lighter or unburdened?

Imagine you are floating in a calm ocean. Feel the water beneath you, the waves gently rocking your body, and the warmth of the sun on your skin. Stay here for as long as you are comfortable, enjoying the scene created by your imagination.

What or who has disappointed you? Bring the circumstances to your mind but imagine you are watching the scene from afar. Does this give you a different perspective on the situation?

Consider how your day is governed by time and the need to "get things done." How would your day differ if you had no concept of time?

Think of a personal achievement. Close your eyes and allow yourself to be immersed in thoughts of this achievement. Let the warm glow envelop you and congratulate yourself once more.

The next time you are in a long line, treat the time you will spend waiting as an opportunity to take a few minutes out of the day. Allow your mind to wander to a place of tranquility.

Take time to be calm in an otherwise busy day. Seek out a quiet spot and allow your mind to be quiet for a few minutes.

Look at a treasured photograph. Allow yourself to travel back to that time, to be present at the moment the photograph was taken.

What advice would you give your younger self?

Are you a risk taker?

What are your biggest fears?

Would friends and loved ones describe you as emotionally open?

Take a few sips of water and remind yourself of the wonder of this natural resource—for hydration, irrigation, and sanitation. Feel the water replenish and revive your body and mind.

The next time you arrive home, take a few minutes to settle into the space. Close your eyes, take a deep breath, and appreciate the comfort of familiarity.

Make your morning routine a mindful one. Listen to the sound of the water as you shower, breathe in the scent of your toiletries as you wash, feel the texture of your clothing as you dress.

How intuitive are you? Do you find it easy to read a situation and predict what will happen next?

Think about the behavior of very small children, who generally act on impulse. When did you last act impulsively and what was the outcome?

Do you procrastinate? Make a list of anything you are putting off and set realistic timeframes to achieve your tasks.

Place your pen in the center of the page and begin moving it in a spiral motion. Notice the movement of your hand and the distribution of ink on the page. Keep going until you reach the edge of the page.

What would you do differently if your actions were without consequence?

Try going a day or two without something you rely on. This might be your cell phone, your caffeine fix, or your regular updates on social media. How did you cope?

_____

_____

_____

_____

_____

_____

_____

_____

_____

_____

_____

_____

_____

_____

_____

_____

_____

_____

Think about what there is too much of in your life. What steps can you take to minimize this?

Do you need a sleep detox? Take time today to prepare yourself and your room for a restful night's sleep. Check the temperature, remove all electronic devices, and ensure your bedding is comfortable. And relax.

What would you like more of?

Are you extravagant?

Are you frivolous with money? Think about the last time you spent more than you'd intended. Was the experience a positive one or did you feel worried or anxious afterwards?

Do you sometimes say "yes" when you really want to say "no" because you think you should? How does this make you feel?

If you could live your life over again, what would you do differently?

Devote a day to recharging your body and mind. Rest, nourish, and be kind to yourself.

Take time to reignite a lost passion. This may be a hobby that has fallen by the wayside, a particular task you find enjoyable, or visiting a place you find restorative.

What does beauty mean to you?

Are you easily distracted?

List your favorite colors and assign an emotion that feels natural to each one. Think about how these colors are present in your home and wardrobe.

When did you last experience pure joy? Think about that experience and allow the emotion to wash over you once again.

Spend time with someone who makes you laugh. Allow yourself to laugh freely without inhibition and note the effects on your body and mind.

Think about the last time you were really surprised. Why was this?
What effect did the surprise have on you?

List five smells you like and your associations with each.

Focus on a part of your body you dislike. Instead of dwelling on the aspects you don't like, think about its function, how it fits together with your other body parts, and how amazing the human body is.

How helpful are you?

What do you regret?

List the greatest lessons you have learnt during your lifetime and reflect on their impact on you as a person.

Scan your body for tension and pain. Do you feel any discomfort? What could you do differently to minimize this?

Sit quietly and focus on your breathing. Feel the air entering your nose and lungs and note the changes in your body as you exhale. Continue mindfully breathing for a few minutes.

How are your energy levels? Are you tired and restless or focused and energized?

Today try to concentrate on one task or activity at a time. Avoid multitasking and allow yourself to focus.

Could you be silent for a whole day? Try it and see.

What would be the greatest gift you could receive right now?

What motivates you?

What does your body need right now?

What are you waiting for?

Are you a good listener?

Do you have any negative habits? If so, what steps could you take to adopt more positive habits?

What are your weaknesses? List them without judgment and remember that no one is perfect.

Have you ever worried about something that didn't happen? Reflect on why you were worried and what the eventual outcome was.

Make a list of skills you'd like to learn and set goals for how you might achieve this.

Who are your favorite people and why?

How good are you at taking responsibility? Do you sometimes feel responsible for the actions of others?

What are you striving for?

What do you wish you'd known when you were younger?

What can you do today to nurture yourself?

Describe your perfect day. Who will you spend time with and what will you do?

List five things that are essential for you to experience good self-esteem.

Think about a time in your life when you have felt strong. Bring those feelings of strength to the front of your mind and allow yourself to re-experience them in this moment.

What's the bravest thing you've ever done?

Who are you?

What have you overcome?

What are you looking forward to? List upcoming experiences or events that you are excited by.

What is a "good day?" For many of us, a good day will be when we've got lots done. But what if a "good day" could be experienced by doing very little?

What thoughts are occupying your mind at present?

If you could go anywhere and experience anything today, what would you choose?

Do you sometimes find it difficult to pay attention?

Take a walk in the rain, even if you usually avoid this! Feel the cool water on your skin, watch the puddles begin to form, and experience your senses being awakened.

What are you good at?

What's the plan?

To what extent are you a confident person?

List the first five things that come to mind when you read the following words:

Sustainability

Authenticity

Community

Spirituality

Has something about your health been bothering you? Make an appointment to see a medical professional today.

The next time you are walking down a busy street, look up. What can you see? Notice the rooftops, the symmetry in the buildings' design, and any patterns created by telephone wires.

Write a letter to someone you have been meaning to thank.

Are you curious? We tend to lose our natural sense of curiosity as we enter adulthood, but try spending a day really exploring everything around you, and see the world through a child's eyes.

How do you decide what to eat? Do you tend to grab snacks on the go? Try really thinking about what your body needs and plan your meals accordingly.

Make a list of problems you have solved.

What excites you?

The next time your phone rings, don't answer it straight away—take a deep breath and count to three to allow your mind to go quiet and prepare to listen.

Are you governed by your head or your heart?

How quickly do you jump to conclusions? The next time you are faced with a new situation or meet someone for the first time, focus on what is in front of you rather than guessing what might be behind the scenes.

The next time you feel a strong emotion such as anger, resentment, or hurt, take a breath and consider how this emotion will affect you. We can't always choose the situations we find ourselves in, but we can choose how we react.

Do you have a tendency to take things for granted? Spend the day appreciating the small things—a bright, crisp morning, the smell of freshly cut grass, a loved one's smile.

How do you engage with other people? If you're guilty of only half paying attention while checking your cell phone or being distracted, try looking the other person directly in the eye and turning your shoulders towards them to give them your full attention.

Tell someone that you appreciate them.

What do you do to relax?

Close your eyes and open a drawer in your home or workplace.
Today is all about celebrating the small things. Feel pride in every small
accomplishment and reward yourself with moments of quiet reflection.

Walk slowly in a circle around the room, looking around you as you walk. Did you notice anything for the first time?

Run your fingers over a piece of paper. Think about how that piece of paper came into being, from tree sapling to notepad. Is there a journey in your own life that resonates with this?

Visualize a flower bud slowly opening to reveal its true beauty. Imagine you are that flower, gradually unveiling, blossoming, and moving toward the light. Note the effect on your mood.

Reflect on a time when you felt courageous. Why was this and how can you channel that energy right now?

Think back to a time when your actions were out of character. What was the outcome? How did others react?

How well do you accept praise? Do you have a tendency to minimize it? Try to accept praise with grace and note the effects on your self-confidence.

Today try to be completely non-judgmental. Assess situations at face-value and take each moment as it comes. Afterward, decide if this was an easy exercise or if you had to keep consciously bringing your mind back to the present.

Imagine you are 10-feet tall. You tower over your peers and are completely conspicuous. How does this make you feel?

How have you evolved?

Are you predictable?

Turn household chores into a mindful experience. Breathe in and appreciate the smell of fresh laundry, notice the changing sounds as water gushes from the faucet, and find pleasure in the orderly home you have created.

What are your mechanisms for maintaining perspective when things go wrong? If you struggle with this, imagine a point in the future and ask yourself how important the current issue will be then.

Immerse yourself in water, either in the tub or at a pool. Slowly move your arms and legs against the resistance of the water, then allow your limbs to float to the surface, and note the feeling of weightlessness.

How satisfied are you with your life right now on a scale of 1 to 10? If the score is lower than you would like, are there any steps you could take to increase your feeling of satisfaction?

What are your strengths? List as many as you can think of, no matter how trivial they may seem. Come back to this list every time you feel you need reminding.

Think of someone who inspires you. List the qualities or achievements you particularly admire and think about how you might emulate them.

What does adoration mean to you?

What energizes you?

Feeling stressed? Take a time out. A few moments to gather your thoughts can have a soothing effect on a frazzled mind.

Give thanks. The next time you appreciate someone's actions, make eye contact and say, "Thank you," with a smile. Did this enhance your feelings of appreciation?

Do you have emotional baggage? Carrying it around can be a drain on your mental resources. Use the space below to write about this and then leave it here, on this page, while you move forward unburdened.

To what extent do you feel in charge of your own destiny? Taking responsibility of your future and being active rather than passive can help with motivation and productivity.

How often do you socialize and how does this affect your mental wellbeing? Fear of missing out can lead us to accept social invitations when our bodies and minds are telling us that this may not be what is needed right now.

Who do you admire?

What are you capable of?

Feeling lethargic? Exercise can be wonderful for increasing energy levels and flooding the body with endorphins. Try exercising for 10 to 15 minutes and note the effects.

The next time you feel like the mental load is too much, make a list of what really matters right now. Is there anything you can offload to be dealt with later, or delegated to someone else who may have more time? Focus on the priorities—anything less important can wait.

Need some headspace? Get outside. A feeling of physical space can do wonders for a busy mind. Take some deep breaths and note the effects of your surroundings on your mental state.

In an ideal world, our bodies and minds would be perfectly balanced at all times to achieve maximum wellness. In reality, there are many factors that challenge the equilibrium. Acknowledge any challenges you are currently facing and take time to consider how the balance could be restored.

How quick are you to complain? If you have a tendency to moan about trivial grievances, stop and try to find a positive in the situation. Did this change your view?

What turned out better than you expected?

What do you find comforting?

List your hopes and dreams, no matter how unachievable or unrealistic they may seem. Now focus on one aspect of each that you may be able to action. For example, a dream of visiting Saturn is likely to be out of reach (at least for now!) but viewing footage taken by the Cassini spacecraft online is only a few clicks away.

Use the space below to write down the greatest piece of advice you've ever been given. How readily have you followed this advice?

How confident are you feeling today? List your confidence boosters and return to this list when you need a reminder.

Set yourself small goals for this week. This could be as simple as unloading the dishwasher before you leave for work in the morning or turning off your cell phone an hour before bed. Congratulate yourself on achieving your goal and see if you can turn this into a habit.

Use the space below to create a weekly mood board. Each day add words, drawings, or cuttings that best represent your mood. Take stock at the end of the week and reflect on which emotions were more prevalent.

What are you winning at?

Who do you confide in?

Appraise your performance. Imagine you are your boss and this is a review meeting. How well would you rate your recent performance and what targets will you set yourself for the coming quarter?

Spend money mindfully. Take a step back and ask yourself if you really need the item or service. Imagine how you will feel tomorrow if you decide not to purchase. If you realize that you are about to spend money on a want rather than a need, walk away and congratulate yourself.

Ask a good friend or trusted relative what they think your best qualities are. Was their answer as you expected or a surprise? How did you feel hearing this?

At times of emotional challenge it can be helpful to focus the mind on what you have to be thankful for. A safe home, a warm bed, and enough food to eat may seem trivial but they are essential for us to thrive. List what you are thankful for right now.

What are you intending to do?

What do you most desire?

How contented are you?

What are your aims?

If you are prone to worrying, set aside a time for this each day. If you feel worried about anything at any other point during the day, remind yourself that this is not the right time and you will have space to worry later.

Today the theme is "you can do this!" Every time you feel self-doubt, remind yourself that this is a day to be bold. Not everything will go your way but allow any mishaps to wash over you. Note how this attitude has affected your day.

The next time you receive a negative comment, try to deal with it in the moment. Letting the comment wash over you or calmly stating why you find the comment hurtful may enable you to move on. Remember that you are in control.

Make a list of activities you find enjoyable and try to incorporate at least one into every day this week.

To what extent are your actions representative of your thoughts?
Take a few minutes to consider this and note any discrepancies.

How well do you accept unfavorable circumstances or situations that are out of your control? Remind yourself that acceptance doesn't equate with agreement, but it may help you to feel more at peace with your position.

How will you make today better?

What do you despise?

Try to eat only when sitting down and pause for a few moments before you take a bite. This will not only avoid the temptation to mindlessly snack but will also help you to really appreciate your food. Note if this makes mealtimes more pleasurable.

Listen to music belonging to three completely different genres (e.g. heavy metal, classical, and hip-hop). Close your eyes to allow yourself to be completely absorbed. Notice the rhythm, tempo, and any recognizable instruments.

Try going to bed one hour earlier than usual following your usual bedtime routine. Repeat for three nights and notice any positive changes to your mood on waking.

Take a few moments to check your attitude. It's all too easy to fall into a habit of feeling a certain way, when a change of attitude may have a positive effect.

What do you need to face up to?

What makes you tick?

Write down your long-term goals. How will you take steps to make them a reality? Can you do something right now to move a little closer to your end-goal?

Try to face at least one of your fears today. You may find that it wasn't nearly as bad as you imagined, and that you had been worrying about something that wasn't going to happen. How was it for you?

Channel your inner introvert. Create a minimally stimulating environment and spend some time alone focusing on your thoughts. Did this come naturally or were you craving social interaction?

Try to stop thinking about the past or the future and focus on the present. You can't change the past or predict the future, but you can make real-time changes to maximize your happiness.

What is the greatest gift you have received?

To what extent are you humble?

What do you do to have fun? We can all too often become bogged down with the monotony of day-to-day life and forget that we need a release. Do something fun today and note how it made you feel.

Smile more. Smiling can help to release feel-good hormones as well as having a positive effect on those around us.

Write how you would react to each of the following situations:

A lion escapes from
a local zoo.

Your mother visits
unexpectedly.

You see your best friend's
partner on a date
with someone else.

The wi-fi connection
at your home
is permanently cut.

How often do you experience jealousy? The next time this emotion arises, try to think rationally about whether the feelings are justified.

Do you often experience feelings of anxiety? Track your anxiety levels over a couple of weeks to get a clearer picture of what may trigger these feelings.

Allow yourself to follow your heart today. If you are a practical person this may not come naturally but try to focus on what your heart desires. Note how this affects your decision-making.

Do you believe in yourself?

What are your ambitions?

Take yourself on an adventure today. This could be as simple as visiting somewhere new in your local area or as daring as heading off on a last-minute vacation. Was this impulsiveness out of character or typical behavior?

How will you practice self-care today? Try to take time, no matter how busy you are, for at least one act of self-care every day.

Focus on increasing your awareness of your body—the space it takes up in the room, how it moves, the weight bearing down on the floor or chair. Think about your internal organs working perfectly in synch without prompts.

Today your mantra is "less is more." Try to un-fill your day rather than keeping busy at all times. Allow time to pass and try to avoid the temptation to "fit more in."

How realistic are your expectations? If your expectations are high you may find yourself experiencing feelings of disappointment when things don't work out as you'd hoped. Use the space below to list any unrealistically high expectations and their more achievable outcomes.

Practice putting yourself first. This can be difficult, especially if you have others who depend on you, but try to focus on having at least some of your needs met today. Note the effects on your sense of wellbeing.

If you find yourself panicking today, close your eyes and repeat, "You are safe, you are safe," until you feel calmer. Note if this enabled you to reassess the situation and approach it with a more relaxed attitude.

What did you enjoy about today?

Are you successful?

Imagine you are walking through a forest. Visualize the beams of light shining through the leaf canopy, the smell of wood and moss, and the sounds of the forest floor underfoot. Stay here for a few moments appreciating the tranquility.

This week magically has an eighth day. How will you spend it?

Step outside at night and look up at the sky. Take a moment to marvel at the universe beyond our atmosphere, the planets and stars, and the man-made satellites orbiting Earth. Appreciate that we are tiny specks in this infinite expanse.

What have you found difficult today? List any experiences you have found tricky. How did you manage these situations and is there anything you would do differently if they arose again?

Would you rather visit a library or a sports club?

Is there an afterlife?

Are you pro-active or reactive?

Set a stopwatch and close your eyes. Without counting, try to guess when one minute has passed. Open your eyes and see how close your estimate was. Repeat this exercise for two and three minutes and consider how we perceive the passing of time.

The next time you find yourself awake at a time when you would usually be asleep, take a few minutes to look around your home and out of the window. Note any changes from how you are used to experiencing your environment.

Take time to notice the birds. Hear their birdsong, watch them in flight, and notice their feathers. Even in urban environments we are usually surrounded by birds but rarely stop to consider them.

Are you doing what you truly want to be doing?

What do you not understand?

Are you free?

What numbers can you see around you as you go about your day? What is their purpose? Think about how numbers are vital for communication and orientation.

List the letters A, B, C, D, and E in the space below then write down a positive word beginning with each letter.

Light a candle. Watch the flame dance and notice the color changes from the center to the outer edges. Allow the candle to burn for a few minutes and see how the wax forms into drips.

What time of year is it? Take a moment to consider the seasonal changes throughout the year. Does the temperature fluctuate much where you live? Is there a difference in the amount of rainfall and hours of daylight?

What makes you unique?

Focus on seeing the good in every person and situation today. If you feel your mind wandering towards negatives, gently bring it back and tell yourself there is good in everyone and everything if you look hard enough.

Use the space below to create your own mini mandala. Don't worry too much about precision—instead enjoy the meditative effects as your pen works to create a labyrinth of shapes and patterns.

Are you held back by "what-ifs?"

Of what are you most proud?

Write down three affirmations that have meaning to you. Then repeat them to yourself several times throughout the day. Note any effects on your mood and state of mind.

Are there obstacles blocking your path to happiness? Close your eyes and imagine the obstacles are hurdles on a race track. Visualize yourself running and jumping over the hurdles and enjoy the feeling of release as you reach the finish line.

Close your eyes and stand on your tip toes with your arms outstretched. Pull your shoulders back and tilt your head slightly upward. Remain in this open-hearted pose for as long as you feel comfortable, enjoying the peace it brings to your body and mind.

How do you communicate? Do you rely on quick text messages or e-mail? Today try to communicate verbally and note how it makes you feel.

How restrained are you?

What does it mean to be alive?

Think about a close relationship. Without judgment, consider whether you are the main giver or taker in the relationship, or if the balance is equal. If there is an imbalance, ask yourself if this can be readdressed.

If peaceful resolution is the answer, what is the question?

When life seems chaotic, stop. Sit or stand still and focus on nothing but the breath entering and leaving your body. The chaos around you may continue but remain still until your mind quiets down.

Set yourself a task of studying the sky for a few minutes at the same time each day for a week. Notice the cloud formations, the light, the shape of the moon (if visible), and any other objects such as birds or airplanes.

Do you have good fortune?

Are you a perfectionist?

Did you know that the letters in the word "listen" can be re-arranged to spell "silent?" The next time you are listening to a friend or relative, focus on their words rather than what to say next.

Look at your face in a mirror. Focus on the shape of your eyes, nose, and mouth. Notice how your face changes shape as you smile and frown.

Look in your closet. Is there an item or outfit you might usually consider too bold or daring for today? Put it on anyway!

Are you easily annoyed by trivial things? Someone pushing past you in the street, rain when you've forgotten your umbrella, finding your favorite lunch spot already occupied? Greet these inconveniences with a smile today.

Does magic exist?

What or who are you avoiding?

Today pick up someone else's litter and throw it in the trash. It may not be your job but think of the benefits to your environment.

Plant a seed or sapling—even the tiniest apartment has space for a small pot. Water it each day and watch your plant grow.

How well do you cope with rejection? Accept that sometimes decisions are made that are beyond your control, and that the rejection isn't necessarily a reflection on you.

Invasions of personal space can be difficult to deal with. Stand firm and politely request that the other person takes a step back. They may not have realized that their closeness was bothering you.

At what could you try harder?

Where are you going?

What can you not be bothered to do?

What makes you laugh?

The next time you feel beaten down, imagine you are surrounded by an impenetrable shield. Visualize yourself inside this protective bubble as you go about your day, deflecting negativity and cynicism.

Ask yourself how fulfilled you are. If the answer is less than you would like, think about any steps you could take right now to feel better.

Feelings of failure can be unpleasant and upsetting. Remember that you are not defined by this outcome and try mentally detaching yourself from the perceived failure.

If you could travel back in time, what would you tell yourself to stop worrying about? What might your future self tell the you of today to worry less about?

What have you settled for?

Is the glass half full or half empty?

Do something today to help out a friend or relative. How did it make you feel?

Imagine you are experiencing everything for the first time. How would your very first glimpse of the sky make you feel? Your first road trip? First embrace with a loved one? Note if this changes your perception of your everyday activities.

You are transported to the place of your dreams. Where are you?

What makes you feel empowered?

What are you irritated by?

Are you an optimist?

Would you choose to spend a rare day off alone or with others?

When the world seems dark, look towards the light. Rise early and watch the sun rise. Reflect on the brand-new day and all its possibilities.

If eyes are the windows to the soul, what do others see when they look into yours?

If you find yourself feeling unfocused and distracted, close your eyes and visualize the tip of a pencil. Keep focusing for the count of ten, then open your eyes and take a deep breath.

Are you bad tempered?

What would you choose: time or possessions?

If you are feeling out of control, make a list of things affecting your life that you have control over then highlight anything that is out of your control. Accept that there are issues and circumstances that you cannot influence, but plenty that you can.

How would you like to grow old?

Look around you—notice how patterns exist in the things we see every day, such as fabric, architecture, and road markings. Do you find the repetition of visual patterns appealing, or are you drawn to more random marks and colors?

What promises have you broken?

Five minutes early or five minutes late?

How do you express yourself?

If today was the end of the world, what would you do?

Imagine you are transported to an environment that is completely the opposite to your own. What changes will you need to make to survive? How will you adapt your daily routine and behaviors?

Would you ever break the law for something you believed in?

Place your hand on your heart. Feel it beating and pumping vital blood, oxygen, and nutrients around your body. Marvel at the wonder of this life-sustaining organ.

Would you rather be over- or under-dressed?

Are you argumentative?

What have you learnt today? How valuable is this knowledge?

If you are about to face a difficult situation, stand tall and imagine you are being pulled towards the ceiling by an invisible force.

How well do you manage disagreements? Remind yourself that we are all individuals and that differences of opinion are a fact of life.

Study your hands. Notice any marks, scars, or lines on the skin.
Think about how valuable your hands are and how many tasks they
complete every day.

Slowly recite the alphabet out loud, exaggerating every sound. Consider the wonder of the spoken word and imagine a world without it.

Glossary

Affirmation: A short positive statement that is repeated over and over with the aim of influencing thoughts or feelings.

Anxiety: Feelings of unease, worry, or fear, particularly about future events.

Apathy: Indifference or lack of engagement with one's environment.

Conflict: An argument or strong disagreement between people with differing opinions.

Criticism: Appraisal or opinion on the actions or merits of someone or something.

Detox: A period of abstinence from something that is having a negative effect.

Empathy: An understanding and awareness of the thoughts and feelings of others.

Intuition: To instinctively understand something without explanation or reasoning.

Judgment: The formation of considered opinions or conclusions.

Mandala: Drawn or painted geometric design emanating from a central point and used as a meditative device.

Meditation: The practice of focusing attention and awareness to achieve mental and emotional clarity.

Pose: A way of moving the body into a certain configuration to achieve a desired shape.

Stress: The body's reaction to feelings of being under pressure or unable to cope.

Visualization: The formation of a mental image of something.

Wellness: Being in a state of good health.